D1506879

920254

DATE DUE

NOV 1 7 1998			
DEC 1 5 2003			

DEMCO

THE ASSASSINATION OF JULIUS CAESAR

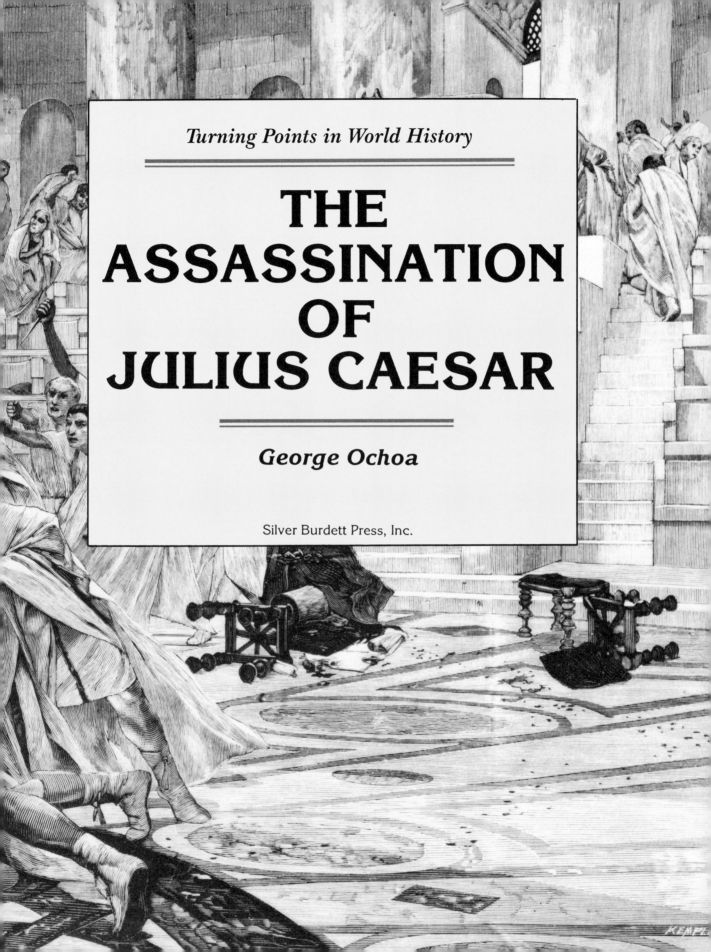

Turning Points in World History

THE ASSASSINATION OF JULIUS CAESAR

George Ochoa

Silver Burdett Press, Inc.

Acknowledgments

The author and editor thank the following people for their invaluable help in text and picture research: Ronald Sheridan and Jaquie Feldman, the Ancient Art & Architecture Collection; Hilary Evans, the Mary Evans Picture Library; and John E. Rosenthal, Rosenthal Art Slides.

Consultants

We thank the following people for reviewing the manuscript and offering their helpful suggestions:

William V. Harris
Professor
Department of History
Columbia College
New York, New York

Carmela V. Metosh, M.A.
High School Latin Teacher and Chairperson of the Foreign
    Language Department, Retired
William Nottingham High School
Syracuse, New York
Past Chairperson of the New York State Teachers of Foreign
    Languages for the Central Zone
Writer of New York State Latin Regents Exams

Cover: Caesar meets his death at the hand of assassins in this nineteenth-century Italian painting. Scala/Art Resource, N.Y.

Title Page: A modern view of Caesar's assassination. Courtesy of the Mary Evans Picture Library.

Contents Page: This Roman coin was minted to mark Caesar's death. One side shows the head of Brutus, one of Caesar's assassins; the other depicts a dagger, a cap symbolizing liberty, and the Latin words Eid. Mar.— *March 15, the date of the assassination.*

Back Cover: A bust of Julius Caesar. Courtesy of Rosenthal Art Slides.

Library of Congress Cataloging-in-Publication Data

Ochoa, George.
    The assasssination of Julius Caesar / George Ochoa.
       p.   cm. -- (turning points in world history)
    Includes bibliographical references and index.
    Summary: Examines the life and violent death of the Roman general
and statesman who founded a line of emperors to inherit his power
and his name.
    1. Caesar, Julius--Juvenile literature. 2. Rome--History-
Republic, 256-30 B.C.--Juvenile literature. 4. Generals--Rome-
-Biography--Juvenile literature. [1.Caesar, Julius. 2. Heads of
state. 3. Generals. 4. Rome--History--Republic, 256-30 B.C.]
I. Title. II. Series.
DG261.024 1991
937'.05'092--dc20
[B]   91-7438
                              CIP
                              AC

Editorial Coordination by Richard G. Gallin

 Created by Media Projects Incorporated

Carter Smith, *Executive Editor*
Charles A. Wills, *Series Editor*
Bernard Schleifer, *Design Consultant*
R.R. Donnelley & Sons Company, *Cartographer*

ISBN   0-382-24130-4 [lib. bdg.]
10 9 8 7 6 5 4 3 2 1

ISBN   0-382-24136-3 [pbk.]
10 9 8 7 6 5 4 3 2 1

CONTENTS

The Royal Crown

It was a cold winter day in 44 B.C., and the people of Rome were celebrating. The day was February 15, the day of the Lupercalia, a festival honoring Lupercus, a god of nature. In a cave at the bottom of Palatine Hill, two teams of priests prepared for the celebration. In the streets above, the people waited to see the priests come out.

The priests—called *Luperci*—were all young men, sons of the noble families of Rome. The leader of one of the teams was Marc Antony, trusted friend of Rome's dictator, Julius Caesar. Normally, Antony wore a toga, a woolen garment like a large white sheet. But today he and the other Luperci shivered in the cold, naked except for goatskins tied around their waists.

The cave still smelled of burning wood, wine, and freshly cooked meat. In the cave, the young priests had sacrificed two goats and a dog, killing them

Like most statues of Julius Caesar, this one shows the Roman leader in a heroic pose.

in honor of Lupercus. Goats were special to Lupercus (who is now better known as Pan or Faunus). People thought of him as having the horns and legs of a goat, with the head and torso of a man. The Romans thought he had the power to protect flocks, help hunters, and promote the birth of children. At the Lupercalia, the Romans asked for his blessings.

In the cave, Marc Antony and the other Luperci smeared their faces with goat's blood. Then, carrying long strips of goatskin, they ran up a racecourse into the streets of Rome. As they ran, they hit the wrists of any woman they saw with the strips of goatskin. People believed that any woman so touched would become pregnant within the year. Women who wanted to have children pressed toward the racecourse. Other Romans watched and cheered.

The finish line for the race was at the Roman Forum. This was a public square surrounded by shops, public buildings, monuments, and temples. On the Rostra, or speakers' platform, Julius Caesar

Animal sacrifices, like the one performed at the Lupercalia, were an important part of Roman religion. Here, priests prepare to sacrifice an ox to assure victory for Rome's legions.

sat on a golden chair and waited for the runners.

Caesar was a balding, broad-faced man of fifty-five. His dark brown eyes were sharp with humor and intelligence. Wrapped in a purple toga, his body was tough from years of military service. He was master of the day's ceremonies. He was also master of Rome.

Rome, a city on the Tiber River in central Italy, ruled nearly every shore of the Mediterranean Sea—from Europe to western Asia to what is now called the Middle East to northern Africa. Caesar's battles had done much to help Rome extend its empire. But his greatest battles had been against Rome itself. He had forced the government to give him the title dictator for life. That meant all of Rome had to obey his commands. As long as he lived, his power was almost unlimited.

The Romans had given Caesar many honors, but they had not given him one: the title king. The Romans took great pride in the fact that they were a republic, a self-governing society. For nearly five hundred years, they had ruled themselves. Even now that they were ruled by a dictator for life, they could not bear to call him king.

At the head of the teams of Luperci, Marc Antony reached the Forum first. He ran up, stopped before the Rostra, and greeted Caesar. Then someone—perhaps Antony, perhaps another of the

Luperci—climbed up onto the platform and placed a crown on Caesar's head. It was a royal crown. It was not part of the festivities.

Antony shouted, "The people offer this to you through me!" The crowd watched, stunned. Some people cried out for Caesar to accept the crown, but most watched in silence. Caesar took off the crown, refusing it. The people cheered.

Twice more the crown was offered to Caesar. Twice more he refused. Each time he refused the crowd applauded, showing their pleasure that he was not allowing himself to be made king. Caesar ordered the crown to be put away, on the statue of Jupiter, king of the gods.

To this day, no one knows for sure whether Caesar wanted the crown or not. Maybe the whole incident was a surprise to him. Maybe he had arranged it with Antony ahead of time. One way or another, people remembered it. Some said the incident proved that Caesar had no desire to be king. Others said he was only biding his time until the moment was right. Some said that even without the kingship, Caesar had already gone too far.

On March 15, 44 B.C., one month after the feast of Lupercus, Julius Caesar was murdered by a band of men who thought he had gone too far. The assassination was a turning point in Rome's history. The Roman Republic was dead, destroyed by Caesar. With Caesar dead, some other form of government had to take his place. Years of war followed, as

Caesar refuses the crown offered to him by Marc Antony.

rival forces fought for power. In 27 B.C., when the fighting was over, Augustus Caesar, the adopted son of Julius Caesar, had won. The Roman Republic, ruled by its citizens, had ended forever. The Roman empire, ruled by emperors, had begun.

This is the story of the life and death of Julius Caesar—and of the founding of the line of emperors who inherited his power and his name.

CHAPTER ONE

The People's Choice

To the Romans who lived centuries after Julius Caesar, the name *Caesar* meant emperor or ruler. In modern times, the *czar* who once ruled Russia and the *kaiser* who once ruled Germany took their titles from the word *Caesar*. But Julius Caesar himself was not born a ruler. His life and actions are what made the name into a title.

Gaius Julius Caesar was born in Rome in 100 B.C. to a family of *patricians*, aristocrats who were descendants of Rome's earliest ruling families. Gaius was the boy's given name. Julius referred to his clan, the Julian clan. Caesar was the name of his father's specific family within the clan.

The family was fairly wealthy, with large estates in the countryside farmed by slaves. Caesar's family lived in a modest but handsome house in the city, in a neighborhood called the Subura.

Like the houses of most wealthy Romans, this house was made up of several rooms with stone floors. The rooms were arranged around a central courtyard, or *atrium*. The roof of the atrium was open and let in air and light. When it rained, water fell into a pool. Fruits and vegetables were grown in a garden at the rear. Shops run by *plebeians*—Roman citizens who were not patricians—opened on the narrow street at the front.

Most of Rome's citizens were plebeians, and most of them were poor. They were blacksmiths, weavers, shoemakers, grocers. They were fullers, who cleaned clothes, and pharmacists, who sold herbs and magic potions for the sick. They were small farmers bringing their goods to market. They were the unemployed and homeless. Most plebeians in the city lived in crowded, dirty apartment buildings. In the country they lived in huts made of sun-dried clay.

Even the poorest plebeian had certain rights as a Roman citizen. For example, plebeians were protected by Roman law courts. They had the right to own property and make contracts. Men (but not

A restored Roman house, showing the atrium, or open central courtyard.

Slavery was widespread in Rome and its territories. Many slaves, like those shown in this later engraving, were captured in battle.

women) had the right to vote. But Rome was also populated by slaves, who had no rights. Slaves were bought and sold like property. Nearly all were foreigners, captured in war or kidnapped by pirates. Educated slaves served in fine homes as tutors or secretaries. Most unskilled slaves worked far from Rome on large farms and construction projects and in mines.

Some plebeians were very rich. They or their ancestors had become wealthy by acquiring land, lending money, or collecting taxes. Any Roman whose wealth was greater than 400,000 sesterces (a very large sum to most Romans) could become an *equestrian*, or knight. Any Roman could run for public office. But only a few were rich enough to pay the high costs of an election campaign. Some families had a history of holding public office and serving in the Senate, Rome's most respected ruling body. These families, whether patrician or plebeian, were considered *noble*, or aristocratic.

Caesar's family was patrician, but it was not as wealthy or influential as other noble families. Caesar's father Gaius had reached the high post of *praetor*, an official in charge of judicial matters, but had not gone on to the highest post—*consul*, or chief executive.

Caesar's mother, Aurelia, like all Roman women, had to stay out of political life. She was expected to obey her husband and take care of her children. She had two daughters to raise besides Caesar. Both were named Julia, in keeping with the Roman tradition of giving all girls the name of the clan. They could never hold public office. But Aurelia had high hopes for her son.

One talent of Aurelia's that influenced Caesar was her gift for speaking clearly and elegantly. Like other Roman aristocrats, Caesar also received training in speaking and writing from a private tutor. In the government of Rome, oratory (speech making) was important. A Roman had to be able to influence others to vote for him or for his policies.

Romans—especially the aristocrats, who held the most power—were proud that they ruled themselves through peaceful debate rather than violence. Caesar voiced a common feeling when he wrote, "I have always reckoned the dignity of the republic of first importance and preferable to life." No monarch forced them to obey; no one was above the law. This was the Roman Republic, the basis of what the Romans called *libertas* (liberty).

In this ceremony, when he was thirteen years old, Caesar was dressed in a toga symbolizing his rights and responsibilities as a Roman citizen.

Rome had not always been a republic. For most of the city's first century (about 600 B.C. to 500 B.C.), the native people of Rome were ruled by conquerors called the Etruscans. The Etruscans placed a king in Rome. Around 500 B.C., the Romans overthrew the Etruscans. Rome never again had a king.

By the third century B.C., the Roman Republic had reached its mature form. It was a democracy because power rested with the people, or at least with male citizens. But it was also an oligarchy, or government by the few, because a small number of people held most of the political power. Most of the republic's institutions were designed to protect

This profile of a Roman woman comes from Herculaneum, a Roman resort town destroyed by a volcano eruption.

the aristocrats and the wealthy, even though some institutions also gave a voice to the poor.

The republic was organized as follows: Rome's adult male citizens met as a group several times a year in two assemblies, the Centuriate Assembly and the Tribal Assembly. Everyone present could vote, but the Centuriate Assembly was largely controlled by the rich. It elected most major officials, or *magistrates*. These included two *consuls,* or chief executives, several *praetors,* in charge of judicial matters, and *quaestors,* in charge of finances.

The poor had more influence over the Tribal Assembly. This assembly elected the ten *tribunes,* or protectors of the plebeians. The tribunes fought for the needs of commoners.

There was one other ruling body in Rome—the Senate. The Senate was made up of about 300 men who met regularly and served for life. All had held public office as magistrates. The Senate controlled Rome's finances and foreign policy and advised on most other matters. Its advice had great influence. By the time of Caesar, the Senate was the most powerful element in the government.

Despite its power, the Senate could not act alone. The Roman Republic was based on a system of checks and balances. Each institution acted as a check, or brake, on the ambitions of the others. For example, Roman magistrates had many powers, but each served only a one-year term. The two consuls had broad powers to run the government, but they had to agree with each other on important matters. The Centuriate Assembly had the power to pass laws, but the Senate could issue its own decrees. The Tribal Assembly could issue legislation called plebiscites. The tribunes could veto, or overturn, any acts of the other institutions.

The republic's system of checks and balances ensured that change came slowly. Peace was usually maintained, even when opinions differed and tempers ran high. In time of emergency, a dictator could be elected. His orders overruled all other laws and decrees. But after six months the dictator was required to step down. The Romans did not want to lose their liberty.

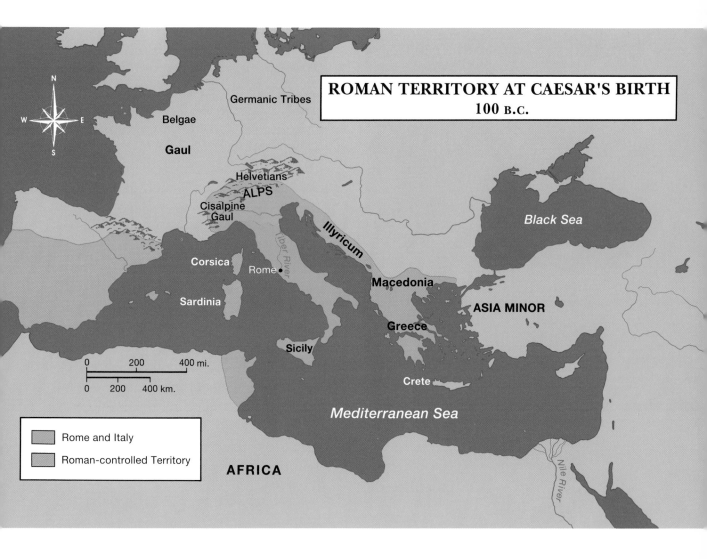

Germanic Tribes

Belgae

Gaul

Helvetians

ALPS

Cisalpine Gaul

Illyricum

Black Sea

Corsica

Rome

Tiber River

Macedonia

Sardinia

ASIA MINOR

Greece

Sicily

Crete

Mediterranean Sea

Nile River

0   200   400 mi.

0   200   400 km.

☐ Rome and Italy
☐ Roman-controlled Territory

AFRICA

The Roman system of government was (and still is) much admired. The ancient Greek historian Polybius called it "a constitution than which it is impossible to find a better." But by the time of Caesar, the orderly workings of the republic had begun to break down. Violence had become a part of the political process. The constitution was in danger of being overthrown. At the root of the disorder was the fact that Rome, once a small city-state, had become the capital of a great empire.

Rome's first conquests had been in what is now Italy. By 275 B.C., Rome had conquered all of the Italian peninsula—the part of Italy that is surrounded by water. In a series of wars in the third and second centuries B.C., Rome's territory grew larger. Sicily, Corsica, and Sardinia (islands off the coast of Italy) and large areas of Spain and North Africa became Rome's. So did the parts of the region called Gaul that are now northern Italy and southern France. Greece, parts of eastern Europe, and part of

Sulla, who became Rome's dictator in 82 B.C.

what is now Turkey also passed under Rome's control.

These lands brought Rome great wealth. The conquered areas—organized as provinces, or subject states—paid taxes in money and in crops such as wheat. Hundreds of thousands of people captured in war were brought to Rome as slaves. Plundered goods became Roman property.

But with new wealth came problems—problems that soon shook Rome to its roots. One problem was landlessness. Before the wars, most Roman citizens had been small wheat farmers. But many lost their farms through neglect while they were fighting Rome's wars.

Wealthy Romans formed large plantations and ranches out of the abandoned plots. Landless Romans found it hard to get work because wealthy Romans preferred to use slaves. Thanks to the wars of conquest, slaves were now cheap and easily obtained.

While these wars made many Romans poorer, they made a few Romans richer. Landowners used their slaves to produce wine and olive oil and raise sheep and cattle. Merchants grew rich on trade. "Tax farmers," hired by Rome to collect taxes in the provinces, became wealthy by collecting more money from subjects than Rome required. Governors of provinces built great fortunes by cheating, robbing, and taking bribes. Cicero, a Roman senator, wrote in 70 B.C., "Because of Roman greed and Roman injustice, all our provinces are mourning, all our free communities are complaining, and even foreign kingdoms are protesting."

The greed of Rome's wealthy classes weakened the republic. Slaves, poor people, and provincial subjects frequently revolted and were put down by force. From 90 to 88 B.C., when Caesar was a child, Rome's allies in Italy rebelled in what was called the Social War. The war did not end until Rome gave citizenship to all people who lived on the peninsula.

Meanwhile, competition grew among the wealthy themselves. The rewards of holding public office were often great. A consul, for example, was usually made *proconsul*, or governor of a province, after his term was over. As proconsul, he could increase his wealth at the expense of provincials—people who lived in the province. If he led a military campaign, he might gain valuable plunder.

As the rivalry among people seeking office became more bitter, their methods became more dishonest. Some politicians paid unemployed mobs to vote for them and support their aims. Some office seekers began to realize that Rome's armies could be used to take power. Rome's armies were mostly composed of poor people who volunteered to serve long terms of enlistment as an escape from poverty. These men were sometimes less loyal to the republic than to the generals who cared for their needs.

One factor in the struggle for power was the reluctance of the Senate to accept change. By the time of Caesar, most senators were members of old families that had been in power for years. The senatorial families tried to block "new men," such as newly rich equestrians, from entering and gaining power. They also resisted the demands of the poor for relief from hunger and landlessness.

Two major political groups arose as a result of this conflict. The Optimates ("the best") were conservatives who wanted to protect the power of the old senatorial families. The Populares ("those of the people") pressed for measures that would help the poor and admit "new men" into the Senate. Many politicians in these groups were unscrupulous men who only wanted power. They would switch sides if that would help their careers.

Marius, Caesar's uncle by marriage and Sulla's rival for power, was forced to leave Rome in 88 B.C.

In 82 B.C., when Caesar was eighteen, he came face to face with the chaos that threatened the republic. That was the year Sulla captured Rome.

Lucius Cornelius Sulla was a patrician and an Optimate. His greatest rival until 86 B.C. had been Marius, a plebeian and Populare who had risen through the ranks of the army to become consul and general. By marrying the sister of Caesar's mother, Marius had become Caesar's uncle.

Marius and Sulla used the armies they led to fight for control of Rome. In 88 B.C., Sulla marched on Rome and forced Marius to leave. Then, while Sulla was away fighting a war in Asia, Marius came back, using his own army to seize power. After Marius died, in 86 B.C., his associate Cinna took over. A marriage was arranged between Cinna's daughter Cornelia and young Caesar. Cinna was then the most powerful man in Rome, so the marriage seemed a good match for Caesar. But in 83 B.C., Cinna's enemy Sulla returned to Italy with an army of 40,000 men.

In 82 B.C., after a bloody battle at the gates of Rome, Sulla became the city's new master. He had himself made dictator, the first in more than one hundred years. Unlike previous dictators, Sulla was not required to step down after six months. For the first time, Rome faced the possibility of being ruled by a dictator for life.

Sulla's first step was to wipe out his opponents in a bloody reign of terror. The names of thousands of political "enemies" were posted in public places. Anyone who murdered these proscribed people received a reward. The property of the victims was then seized by the state. Some of the proscribed citizens had committed no other crime than that of being wealthy. Sulla needed their estates so he could pay his soldiers.

Caesar was ordered to come before Sulla. Because of his family connections, he could have been executed. But Sulla was willing to be lenient. He told Caesar he could live, as long as he divorced his wife, Cornelia, Cinna's daughter. Many ordinary men would have obeyed. But Caesar did not. Perhaps because he loved his wife, perhaps because he did

not like Sulla, he refused to divorce Cornelia. He stayed married to her until her death in 69 B.C.

Caesar became an enemy of the state and was forced to go into hiding. With the help of his family, he left Italy. He served with the Roman governor of Asia and returned to Rome only after Sulla had died in 78 B.C. Before retiring from the dictatorship, Sulla had put in place many measures to increase the power of the Senate. Most of these changes did not last, but Sulla's example did. He had used armed force to seize control of Rome. He had ruled it as a dictator. His example showed that violence could be used as a way of gaining autocratic power—an example Caesar would not forget.

After Sulla's death, Caesar studied public speaking and philosophy in Greece. He also tasted battle when he was captured by pirates during one of his journeys. After being ransomed by his relatives, Caesar gathered some ships, found the pirates, and had them crucified. He showed a talent for leadership—and a readiness to use deadly force.

Caesar was brave, intelligent, and skilled in oratory, an impressive young man. But to advance in politics, he needed more than personal ability. He needed powerful friends. By 70 B.C., the most powerful men in Rome were its two consuls—Marcus Licinius Crassus "the Rich" and Gnaeus Pompey "the Great."

Crassus "the Rich" got his nickname because he was one of the wealthiest men in Rome. Pompey "the Great" got his nickname as a talented general under Sulla. Crassus gained military fame by crushing a slave revolt led by a gladiator (professional fighter) named Spartacus. But as a general, Pompey was far more famous. He freed the Mediterranean Sea of the pirates who had been attacking ships and coastal cities. He defeated the Asian king Mithridates. In the Middle East, he conquered Palestine and Syria. His victories pushed the borders of the Roman Empire farther than ever before.

Pompey was a hero of the common people. His army was devoted to him. But the Senate feared that he would use his army and popularity to become another dictator. Crassus feared him as a rival. To strengthen his own position, Crassus allied himself with Caesar.

Crassus saw that Caesar could one day become as popular as Pompey. With Crassus's money and support, Caesar was elected as *aedile*, or city magistrate, in 65 B.C. As a Populare, the thirty-five-year-old Caesar worked hard to win the favor of the common people. He used Crassus's money to provide sports events and other spectacles for the people's entertainment. In 63 B.C., Caesar became *pontifex maximus*, or high priest, in charge of public sacrifices and festivals. In 62 B.C., he became praetor and, in 61 B.C., governor of a province in Spain.

Caesar and Crassus had powerful enemies in the Senate. One was Cato the Younger, a stern, sober Optimate who opposed almost all demands for change.

This pottery fragment bears a profile of the Roman senator Cato the Younger.

Another was Marcus Tullius Cicero, an equestrian who believed strongly in protecting the Roman constitution. Cicero put his beliefs into action in 63 B.C. when he exposed a plot by a patrician named Catiline to overthrow the government.

Cicero wanted to protect the "liberty" of the upper classes to rule Rome in accordance with law and tradition. He believed the Optimates were the faction of "every good man" and the Populares the faction of the worst. "Storms are stirred up in the republic," he said, "so that the men who have claimed for themselves the helm of the country

Cicero, renowned for his ability as an orator, speaks before the Roman Senate.

must keep watch and strive with all their skill and with all their diligence."

Cicero was regarded by his fellow Romans as the greatest orator of his time. To this day, his speeches are considered masterpieces of the Latin language. Under the leadership of Cato and Cicero, the Senate grew hostile to all three of Rome's popular leaders—Pompey, Crassus, and Caesar. On Pompey's return to Rome in 62 B.C., the Senate refused to give his veterans the land he had promised them. The Senate blocked legislation that Pompey and Crassus had pushed for. The Senate discouraged Caesar from running for the office of consul.

In 60 B.C., the three men—Pompey, Crassus, and Caesar—met and formed an informal group that became known as the First Triumvirate. These men, who might otherwise have been rivals, pledged to help one another to gain their political ends. They decided the first step was to help Caesar become consul.

Bribes were paid to voters; deals were struck with the powerful. Caesar promised laws that would favor the equestrians and give relief to the poor. Caesar's personal popularity did the rest. Caesar was elected as one of the two consuls for 59 B.C. Chosen by the people, Caesar took his seat in the highest public office that then existed in Rome.

But this was only the beginning. In time he would create an office that had never yet existed.

CHAPTER TWO

The Rebel

Caesar's consulship in 59 B.C. was marked by violence and lawlessness. Under the Roman constitution, he was supposed to seek the Senate's advice and share power with his fellow consul. But Caesar soon decided not to follow the constitution.

Caesar's first clash with the Optimates came over his land bill or proposed law. The purpose of the bill was to provide plots of land for Pompey's soldiers and for unemployed Romans. Optimate senators felt the bill was a threat to wealthy landowners. When the Senate refused to discuss the bill, Caesar took it directly to the people's assembly.

At the assembly meeting in the Forum, Caesar's fellow consul, an Optimate named Marcus Calpurnius Bibulus, told the people that he would use his veto power to defeat the land bill. "You will not have the law this year," he said, "not even if you all want it." But Bibulus's veto went against the wishes of

A nineteenth-century German print shows Roman soldiers of Caesar's day.

the poor citizens and the soldiers. It also went against the wishes of the powerful leaders of the Populares—Caesar, Crassus, and Pompey.

The day came for the assembly to vote on the land bill. Three tribunes vetoed the bill. Bibulus, accompanied by the conservative senator Cato, spoke out against it. That was enough. An armed mob attacked Bibulus and the three tribunes. Some members of the mob, if not all, had been placed there by Caesar. Cato was carried off. Bibulus had a basket of excrement dumped on his head.

After order had been restored, a vote was taken. Caesar's land bill was passed. From that day on, the Senate stopped fighting Caesar's legislation. Bibulus stayed at home for his own safety, but every day he announced that the omens (signs of the gods' wishes) were unfavorable for public business. Technically, this meant that all Caesar's actions that year were illegal.

Caesar had not carried out a bloodbath. He had not captured Rome by force. But he had used violence to force his opponents to obey him. He had shown no regard for the Roman constitution—or the liberty of the Romans who disagreed with him.

Some of the laws Caesar introduced in his year as consul were meant to please Pompey and Crassus. Pompey's reorganization of the eastern Mediterranean provinces was ratified. Another law gave relief to some equestrian friends of Crassus who collected taxes in Asia for Rome. Tax collectors at that time agreed to pay Rome a certain amount and kept whatever else they could collect. This law lowered the amount they had to pay. Other laws gave public land to poor Roman families and cracked down on dishonest provincial governors.

The Optimates planned to turn against Caesar at the first opportunity. They were not allowed to bring charges against him while he was in an official position. But once he was out of office, they planned to put him on trial for using violence to pass the laws.

Caesar did not allow himself to fall into their hands. Before leaving the consulship, he made sure that he would step directly into a new office—that of *proconsul*, or governor of a province. As proconsul, he would have the chance to collect riches from the province and raise an army. An army would allow him to gain fame and treasure in battle. It might also help him enforce his power in Rome.

The Senate assigned Caesar the provinces of Cisalpine Gaul (now northern Italy) and Illyricum (now part of Yugoslavia). When the governor of Transalpine Gaul (now southern France) died, Caesar arranged to govern that province as well.

Caesar made sure that his friends were placed in government positions to look after his interests while he was away. He strengthened his political alliances with marriage ties. Pompey married Julia, Caesar's daughter. Caesar himself married Calpurnia, the daughter of a wealthy plebeian who succeeded Caesar as consul.

Calpurnia was Caesar's third wife. (His second, Pompeia, he had divorced in 62 B.C.) Little is known about Calpurnia. Roman women were supposed to lead quiet lives, managing the household and raising children. As an aristocrat, she was probably trained as a girl in subjects like rhetoric (speaking and writing) and music. Caesar had many love affairs during his marriage to Calpurnia, but their marriage lasted until he died. The two never had children.

Caesar left in 58 B.C. for Transalpine Gaul. He was not to return to Rome until 49 B.C. In the nine years he was away, he conquered new territories for Rome in the series of conflicts known as the Gallic Wars.

Rome's enemies in the Gallic Wars were the inhabitants of free Gaul—the large section of Gaul that was then independent of Rome. The present-day territories that were then part of Gaul are all of France (except for what the Romans already held), all of Belgium, and parts of Switzerland, Germany, and the Netherlands. When Caesar arrived

Warriors of Gaul. Their clothes and hair appeared alien and frightening to the Roman soldiers. But despite their legendary courage, the Gauls eventually faced defeat at the hands of Rome's skilled, disciplined legions.

with his army at Lake Lemanus in Transalpine Gaul (now Lake Geneva in Switzerland), he was at the northern boundary of Rome's empire. North of him was free Gaul, which Rome wanted for its natural wealth and trade goods. But the Gauls did not want to surrender it.

The Gauls were proud and independent people. They were farmers, herders, craft workers, and warriors. To the Romans, Gallic warriors looked frightening and barbaric. They had long hair and long mustaches. They wore trousers instead of tunics. Their helmets were crowned with animal horns. They were brave and skillful fighters.

But the Gauls had a flaw: They were divided among themselves. As Caesar noted in his memoir, *Commentaries on the Gallic Wars*, the Gauls were composed of at least three different ethnic groups—

Each Roman legion carried a standard symbolizing Rome's authority. The letters SPQR stand for the Latin words Senatus Populusque Romanus—*"The Senate and People of Rome."*

Roman soldiers—equipped, like the one in this picture, with shield, spear, and short sword—were perhaps the best fighters of the ancient world.

the Aquitanians, the Celts, and the Belgians. "All of these have different languages, customs, and laws," wrote Caesar. These groups were divided further into many tribal states, such as the Arvenians and the Helvetians. "Not only every tribe," wrote Caesar, ". . . but almost every family, is divided into rival factions."

The Roman army had the unity that the Gauls lacked. The army was composed of legions—units of up to 6,000 men. Each legion had a standard, or sign, in the shape of an eagle, which the soldiers carried proudly. The legionaires volunteered to serve for many years. In return, they received both pay and the chance for plunder. When they retired, they were given land on which to settle. The legionnaires trained hard, becoming skilled with the spear and the short Roman sword. They also became disciplined, able to march for long distances and hold their ground when defeat seemed near.

War was not only won by foot soldiers. Just as important to Roman success were the works of engineers—bridges, assault towers, catapults, battering rams. These were especially important when laying siege to a fortress—surrounding and starving it until the inhabitants gave up or were taken by force.

Caesar first ventured into free Gaul to win a victory against the Helvetians, a tribe he claimed was dangerous to Rome. He also defeated Ariovistus, an invading chief from Germany, a region to the east of Gaul. Many Gallic tribes began to see Caesar as a threat, and they organized attacks on him. In 57 B.C., Caesar went to war with an alliance of the Belgian tribes of northeast Gaul.

Most of these tribes were fairly easy for the Roman legions to defeat. But one tribe, the Nervii, was a challenge. These determined warriors almost wiped out the Romans during a long battle on the banks of the Sambre River. Just when things looked darkest for the Romans, Caesar drew a sword and fought side by side with his men. He wrote that this action "gave the men fresh heart and hope; each man wanted to do his best under the eyes of his commander-in-chief, however desperate the peril." Caesar's personal bravery in battle became part of his legend—and one of the reasons his troops were so loyal.

By the end of 57 B.C. Caesar's legions had conquered what are now Belgium, the Netherlands, and the parts of France called Normandy and Brittany. His victories were honored in Rome with periods of celebration called public thanksgivings. Captive Gauls were sent to Rome as slaves. So were treasures of gold and silver. The Gauls were subjected to slavery, taxes, and hardship. In the coming years many of these tribes revolted. Caesar, whose proconsulship was extended another five years, stopped every revolt. His armies also made raids into Germany and the distant island of Britain.

Caesar's methods were often brutal, even by the standards of his day. It is estimated that he caused as many as a million deaths in Gaul. In one encounter in 55 B.C., he wiped out two German tribes, sending out his cavalry to hunt down women and children.

The most serious challenge to Roman rule came from Vercingetorix, leader of the Arvenian tribe, who asked the Celts of central Gaul to put away their differences and unite as a single nation. In 52 B.C., the tribes listened to him and formed a mighty confederation under his command.

Vercingetorix used a "scorched earth"

Vercingetorix surrenders to Caesar after the Roman victory at Alesia.

strategy against the Romans. The Celts burned their own towns and fields so that their enemies had nothing to live on. Gallic warriors harassed Roman troops in hit-and-run raids. But not all the Gauls wanted to burn their towns. One tribe insisted on keeping their beautiful hilltop town of Avaricum. Surrounding it with trenches and towers, the Romans captured it in a month.

The final battle came at Vercingetorix's fortress of Alesia. The fortress was protected by hills and streams and seemed impossible to capture. Caesar laid siege to it. His soldiers built miles of defense works—among the most elaborate ever seen in the ancient world. The works included trenches filled with water and pits with stakes to trap the attackers.

The defense works were soon tested from two sides: from the rear by a large Celtic army and from the front by warriors from the town. After several days of hard fighting, Caesar's troops routed the enemy. The next day, Alesia surrendered. Vercingetorix, the great rebel, gave himself up and was put in chains. His revolt was over.

Caesar showed no mercy as he continued to put down scattered revolts. In 51 B.C., his legions captured a fortress called Uxellodunum. Caesar ordered the prisoners set free—with their hands cut off. The handless rebels would be a warning to other Gauls. The Gauls hardly needed more warnings. After years of war and suffering, they were ready to give in.

Roman Gaul now stretched north to the North Sea, west to the Atlantic Ocean, east to the Rhine River. Many centuries later, as Gaul evolved into the nation called France, it would carry Roman influence into the Middle Ages and modern times.

Caesar's conquests also had important effects for him personally. He had built up an army of over 50,000 loyal men. He had won wealth that he used to buy political influence in Italy and overseas. He had gained a reputation as a brilliant general—one who struck hard and fast, planned intelligent strategy, and knew how to get the best from his troops. His reputation was spread in part by his own *Commentaries*, written during his years in Gaul.

Meanwhile, things had not stood still in Rome. The triumvirate of Caesar, Crassus, and Pompey, which had informally ruled Rome for several years, was gone. Pompey had come to see Caesar as a dangerous rival. He was jealous of Caesar's military fame. The marriage link between the two men was broken in 54 B.C., when Pompey's wife, Julia, died. The First Triumvirate ended for good in 53 B.C. at the battle of Carrhae, near what is now the border between Turkey and Syria. There Crassus, then governor of Syria, was killed in a stunning victory by the Parthian Empire, Rome's rival for power in the Middle East.

Rome itself had fallen into chaos. Armed gangs hired by warring political factions fought in the streets. Looking for a strong leader, the Optimates gradually convinced Pompey to turn against Caesar and join their side.

A later depiction of Caesar's crossing of the Rubicon River.

Caesar planned to step directly from his governorship in Gaul into another term as consul in Rome. That way, he would avoid being arrested for what he had done in his earlier term as consul. But the Optimates in the Senate wanted Caesar to give up his command in Gaul and return to Rome as a private citizen. Law and tradition were on their side. A governor had to disarm his troops before returning to Rome and had to be present in Rome to stand for public office. But Caesar's allies in the Senate blocked every move to make Caesar give up his army. The debate grew bitter.

Camped in Cisalpine Gaul north of Italy, Caesar tried to reach an agreement with Pompey and the Optimates. The negotiations failed. In January, 49 B.C., the Senate ordered Caesar to disarm his troops and return to Rome. They ordered Pompey to go and bring him back by force if he refused.

The choice was Caesar's now. He could accept the authority of the Senate and give up his troops, or he could start a civil war. If he returned to Rome without his army, he might well be executed or banished. But if he returned to Rome in force, he might destroy the republic.

No one knows for sure why Caesar made the decision he did. Some think he acted in what he thought were the best interests of Rome. Some think he had no motive but his own ambition. One Roman historian suggested that "constant exercise of power gave Caesar a love of it." In any case he made his choice.

Caesar ordered his single legion in the area—the loyal, battle-hardened Thirteenth Legion—to meet him at the border between Cisalpine Gaul and Italy. A little stream called the Rubicon marked where the border lay. Roman law forbade a provincial governor to enter Italy with his army. The moment Caesar crossed the Rubicon, he would become a rebel against Rome.

Caesar and his army reached the bridge over the stream at dawn on January 11, 49 B.C. Legend has it that he hesitated and said to his staff, "Even yet we may draw back, but once across that little bridge and the issue rests with the

A portrait of Pompey. Once Caesar's partner in the triumvirate that ruled Rome, he became his enemy while Caesar was in Gaul.

sword." Then he called out, "The die is cast!"—the words a gambler would call when throwing dice. Caesar ordered his army to cross the Rubicon. The issue now rested with the sword.

CHAPTER THREE

The Dictator

Italy fell to Caesar with hardly a battle. Once his men were across the Rubicon, they marched along the eastern coast of Italy, capturing town after town. Most of the towns opened their gates wide to Caesar. Many Italians were tired of the Optimates' hold on power. Poor Italians saw Caesar as a hope for social reform. Caesar made himself more popular by his mercy toward the captured towns. His soldiers did not loot or destroy. Local leaders who opposed him were allowed to go free.

As news of Caesar's march spread to Rome, the consuls and most of the senators fled the city. Pompey, who had not yet finished raising an army, was taken off guard. Pompey was a capable general, but he was slow and cautious. Caesar, by contrast, was becoming famous for the speed with which he moved his armies.

In this seventeenth-century portrait, Caesar holds a scepter, symbolizing his power as Rome's dictator.

All hope was not lost for Pompey. In the eastern Mediterranean—in Greece, Asia, and the Middle East—Pompey had rich and powerful allies. They were loyal to him from the days when he fought campaigns in those regions. By drawing on the wealth and manpower of the East, Pompey felt sure he could defeat Caesar.

In March, 49 B.C., with whatever soldiers he could gather, Pompey escaped by ship for the Roman province of Macedonia (now Albania, southern Yugoslavia, and northern Greece). The consuls and many senators went with him. They hoped to come back one day in triumph and carry out procriptions as Sulla had done. They would execute Caesar's supporters and take their property.

Caesar's policy, however, was one of clemency, or mercy. He had shown in Gaul that he was capable of cruelty to foreigners. But he believed in treating his fellow Roman citizens kindly. If they surrendered, he would leave them and

Roman sea power in the Mediterranean was based on galleys like this one, which used both sails and oars.

their property alone. This policy encouraged many former enemies to join his side. But other men he pardoned went on to fight him again.

Caesar entered Rome on April 1, 49 B.C. He was now master of the city, but his position was far from strong. In the west, Spain was controlled by Pompey's lieutenants. In the east, Pompey was mustering a large army. Rome depended on grain supplies from Africa, Sicily, and Sardinia that could easily be cut off. The entire Mediterranean Sea was patrolled by Pompey's ships.

Caesar acted quickly. He sent armies to secure Rome's grain supplies. He himself led the assault on Spain. Within

forty days, he had defeated Pompey's lieutenants. By the end of 49 B.C., he was back in Rome. He arranged to have the Senate appoint him as dictator for eleven days—long enough to get himself elected as one of the two consuls for 48 B.C.

Even though he had won this consulship by force, Caesar now claimed that he was the "legitimate" representative of Rome. He regarded Pompey and the Optimates as the rebels. Still, it was up to Caesar to support his claim with the sword.

In Macedonia, Pompey was preparing for war. He had gathered nine legions of soldiers, with two more on the way.

His allies in the East had sent him soldiers, warships, and money. Soon, Pompey planned to invade Italy and take back Rome.

Caesar did not give him time. At sunset on January 4, 48 B.C., Caesar and seven legions set sail from Italy to Macedonia. His chief lieutenant, Marc Antony, followed later with more legions. Once united, Caesar and Antony laid siege to the port city of Dyrrachium. The siege lasted for months. But Caesar's army was finally driven off by Pompey's forces.

Pompey was now sure of victory. But Caesar was not yet defeated. He rallied his army and marched east—going deeper into Macedonia. He was betting that Pompey would follow him, instead of going on to Italy and recapturing Rome. He was right.

On August 9, 48 B.C., the two armies met near a village called Pharsalus in what is now central Greece. Pompey had 47,000 infantry; Caesar had only 22,000. Pompey's 7,000 cavalry outnumbered Caesar's horsemen seven to one. But Caesar's army was more experienced and better trained, and Caesar was a better general. Caesar used a hidden line of men with spears to drive off Pompey's cavalry. He kept a reserve of soldiers behind the front lines to attack Pompey's army at a critical moment. In one of the most decisive battles in history, Pompey's army was utterly defeated. Caesar's strategy and tactics at Pharsalus are still studied as classics of military art.

Pompey fled the battlefield and sailed away from Macedonia. For him, the war with Caesar was over. He sailed from country to country, looking for one that would give him safe harbor. Caesar followed Pompey, hoping to capture him. Finally, the king of Egypt agreed to let Pompey come ashore. As Pompey landed, he was stabbed in the back and killed. The king's advisers had decided that Pompey was too dangerous to keep alive.

When Caesar landed in Egypt three days later, the king's advisers gave him Pompey's head as a gift. Caesar, who had once been Pompey's friend, wept when he saw it.

While Caesar was in Egypt, he took the time to settle a civil war between the two reigning monarchs—a thirteen-year-old boy named Ptolemy XIII and his older sister Cleopatra VII. The result was a brief conflict known as the Alexandrian War (after Alexandria, then the capital of Egypt). By the end of March, 47 B.C., Caesar had forced a settlement to the war. The boy-king Ptolemy was dead, drowned in the Nile River while trying to escape Caesar's army. Cleopatra, now an ally of Caesar's, was on the throne.

Cleopatra and Caesar had become more than allies. They had also become lovers. He was fifty-two and she was twenty-one when they met. But each found the other brave, intelligent, witty, and attractive. They had one great thing in common: both wanted to rule. In time Cleopatra bore Caesar a son, popularly known as Caesarion, or "little Caesar."

A nineteenth-century view of the Siege of Alexandria in 47 B.C.

In June, 47 B.C., Caesar left Egypt. After a brief stop in Asia to defeat an invading king named Pharnaces, he came back to Rome, where disorder had broken out. Caesar had left Marc Antony in charge of Italy, but Antony had not governed well. Antony was a good soldier but a weak political leader. Many people disapproved of him because he drank too much, spent money lavishly, and had many mistresses. Caesar removed him from power and took charge himself, serving as dictator for the second time. He soon restored peace among rebellious citizens and mutinous troops.

It was in the Roman province of Africa (now part of Tunisia) that the Optimates had gathered for their last stand. Metellus Scipio, Pompey's father-in-law, had mustered an army of 50,000 soldiers. He was helped by Juba, king of the Roman client state of Numidia (which stretched from what is now Algeria to Libya). In April, 46 B.C., the Optimate forces clashed with Caesar at Thapsus on the African coast. The Optimates lost. Numidia became the Roman province of New Africa. Caesar, once again, had defended his claim to power.

When Cato, the most stubborn of

A later artist painted this depiction of a victory parade, one of the events that marked a Roman triumph.

Caesar's enemies, heard the news, he killed himself. He preferred to die rather than accept Caesar's pardon. Few other Optimates were so devoted to their cause. When Caesar returned to Rome in July, 46 B.C., friends and former enemies alike joined in cheering him. No one in Rome could any longer doubt that Caesar was their master.

Caesar was again elected dictator, this time for ten years. The Senate voted him many honors. He was given the right to offer his opinion first in all Senate debates. A public thanksgiving of forty days was declared for his victory in Africa. Four triumphs were held to celebrate his victories. A triumph was a spectacular public and religious celebration, held to honor a general who had won a war. The festivities included joyous military parades and public games. Caesar's triumphs were among the grandest ever held.

Still, Caesar ruled only as long as his armies could keep the peace. In the provinces of Spain, the peace had been broken. Refugees from Africa, including Pompey's two sons, had gathered in Spain for yet another "last stand" against Caesar. Caesar's army clashed with the Pompeians at Munda on March 17, 45 B.C. Caesar won, and the rebellion was defeated. But it was the most savage and hard-fought battle of his career. It was also, though he did not know it, his last.

Caesar returned to Italy, where he readily accepted fresh honors. Statues of Caesar were raised in every temple. His image was stamped on Roman coins. Caesar claimed the right to cover his body with a purple toga, a symbol of royalty, and cover his head with a wreath of laurel leaves, a symbol of victory. He also took on the title *imperator*. It is the root of our modern word *emperor*, though at the time it meant "commander-in-chief." It was used to honor victorious generals. Caesar received the title for life.

The most important title for Caesar, however, was that of dictator. In February, 44 B.C., he was made dictator for life. His power was now nearly unlimited for as long as he lived. Many of the institutions of republican government survived in outward form. But no one in the government had power to overturn his decisions. Senators, consuls, tribunes, and every other official served at his pleasure.

As it turned out, Caesar had little time to use his vast power. Still, some of the changes he enacted were long-lasting. He took land away from people in the provinces to found Roman colonies. Veterans and poor citizens settled in these colonies. This program reduced the numbers of unemployed people in Rome. It also helped to spread Roman culture—and strengthen Roman control—throughout the empire.

Caesar also started a program of public works. These works relieved unemployment and made the city more beautiful. They included a magnificent hall for the law courts, called the Basilica Julia, and a new city square, called the Forum Julium. He tried to reform Rome's administration, by increasing the number of senators and magistrates and reorganizing the government of Italian towns. He helped strengthen ties with the provinces by giving Roman citizenship to many provincials.

Caesar's most lasting reform was the introduction of a new calendar. It was based on the sun instead of the moon, and was far more accurate than the old one. With minor corrections added in the Renaissance, it is the calendar we use today. As yet another honor, the Senate named the month of Julius Caesar's birth "July."

Caesar was a capable and merciful dictator. But some Romans could not forgive him for being dictator at all. They had not forgotten the Roman concept of liberty. They believed that Romans should govern themselves. Some were upset that they could no longer compete freely for power. Some were angry at Caesar's arrogance, or pride. At one point he said sarcastically to a tribune who had refused to honor him, "Hey, there, Aquila the tribune! Do you want me to restore the Republic?"

Rumors began to spread that Caesar wanted to be king. To Romans, kingship was the most hated of all institutions. At least dictatorship had some place in the constitution: The Senate was allowed to name a dictator for a short time. But a king was a ruler who acted as if power was his by right and who passed his power on to an heir. Caesar did not help matters by bringing Queen Cleopatra to live near him in a villa outside Rome. There she received visitors and displayed their royal son, Caesarion.

This portrait coin of Caesar bears the inscription Caesar Dict, *showing that it was minted while Caesar was Rome's dictator.*

Caesar denied that he was interested in kingship. He refused the crown that Antony offered him at the festival of the Lupercalia on February 15, 44 B.C. But the rumors continued.

Caesar's enemies had learned they could not defeat him in war. But perhaps he could be assassinated. Sometime in 44 B.C., men in Rome began talking seriously about murdering Caesar. One of the leaders of these men was Gaius Cassius Longinus. Cassius was one of Pompey's generals. He had been pardoned by Caesar after the battle of Pharsalus. Like many Romans, he hated Caesar as a tyrant (a ruler with unlimited power). He was also angry at Caesar for not advancing him more quickly through the ranks of the government.

Marcus Junius Brutus.

Another leader of the conspiracy was Marcus Junius Brutus. He, too, had opposed Caesar at Pharsalus and had been pardoned. Brutus was a serious, scholarly man. He was respected by his fellow Romans for his high moral character. His mother was Servilia, a mistress of Caesar, and Caesar had great affection for him. Caesar had given him the important office of city *praetor* (judicial magistrate). Brutus may even have been Caesar's son. But Brutus had believed so strongly in Roman liberty that he had fought against Caesar in the civil war. Although Brutus had been roundly defeated, he was still uneasy.

According to legend, one of Brutus's ancestors had helped to drive out Rome's kings. That ancestor was also named Brutus. In 44 B.C., the younger Brutus began to receive unsigned notes saying, "You are asleep, Brutus" and "You are not a true Brutus." Cassius tried to convince him to follow in his ancestor's footsteps and do away with Rome's tyrant. Brutus finally agreed.

There were about sixty conspirators in all. Some joined the conspiracy for noble reasons, some for selfish ones, some because they held personal grudges. Decimus Brutus and Gaius Trebonius, former generals of Caesar, were ambitious for power. One conspirator, Tullius Cimber, was angry because Caesar had exiled his brother, that is, had forced him to leave Rome. All believed they were being faithful to Roman tradition, which made the killing of tyrants an honorable act.

The conspirators knew they had little time. Caesar was planning to leave Rome in March for yet another war. This time, he was planning to fight the Parthian Empire, which was giving aid to a rebellion in the Roman province of Syria.

Caesar had heard rumors of assassination plots, but he was not very concerned. He had even dismissed his bodyguard of two thousand men. Caesar was fifty-five now, his face deeply lined. He was bothered by fits of epilepsy, which left him helpless and shaking at unexpected times. Still, death held no terrors for him. On the last evening of his life, he is said to have remarked to his friends at dinner that the

Caesar's wife, Calpurnia, tells her husband she dreamed of his death.

best kind of death was a sudden one.

Years later, Roman historians reported that there were many strange omens, or signs from the gods, in the days before Caesar died. Sacred horses shed tears. A bird was torn to pieces by other birds. Caesar's wife, Calpurnia, dreamed that her husband was brutally murdered. A fortuneteller warned Caesar to beware the Ides of March—the fifteenth day of the month.

Whether any of these signs took place or not, Caesar did go out into the city on March 15, 44 B.C. He went to the theater built by his old enemy Pompey during one of Pompey's terms as consul. The Senate was meeting that day in a hall next to the main arena.

The senators rose to greet him as he walked into the hall. He sat down on his golden chair near the statue of Pompey. He wore his laurel wreath and his

A later engraving depicts Caesar's assassination in the Senate.

purple toga and carried a stylus, a sharp writing instrument. A group of senators pressed close around him, as people often did to ask him for favors or advice. One of them, Tullius Cimber, asked Caesar to bring his brother back from exile, but Caesar refused.

As a sign to the other assassins, Cimber grabbed Caesar's purple toga and pulled it down off his shoulder. "This is violence!" Caesar cried. A dagger struck him at the base of the neck. It was wielded by a tribune named Casca. Caesar was stunned, but he reacted at once, stabbing Casca's arm with his stylus. Another knife hit Caesar in the side. The old soldier began to fight for his life.

But there were too many assassins, too many knives. Time after time they stabbed him—Cassius, Decimus Brutus, Trebonius—men he had pardoned, men he had trusted. They stabbed him in the chest, in the face, in the legs. It is said that just before he died he saw Marcus Brutus, whom he had loved like a son, drive home another dagger. Some say that Caesar's last words were, "You too, child?"

Covering his head with his toga, Julius Caesar sank to the ground at the foot of Pompey's statue. The man who had started and won the long civil war was dead. With his death, Rome faced civil wars more violent than any before.

CHAPTER FOUR

The New Caesar

In the first hours after Caesar's death, Rome was in chaos. The senators fled the Theater of Pompey, afraid that the assassins would kill them next. People in the streets heard the news and ran home in fear. Red with Caesar's blood, the assassins marched into the Forum, crying "Liberty!" But the Forum was empty. Nearly everyone had fled.

The assassins hadn't thought about what would happen after Caesar's death. They had hoped only to restore the Republic: to put the Senate and the magistrates back in charge. But the Republic had been destroyed by the misrule of the senatorial families and by men like Caesar who used violence to gain power. Caesar had at least put an end to fighting within the government. With Caesar gone, there was no government to take his place.

The consul Marc Antony was the first to try to bring order to the confusion.

Caesar's adopted son, Augustus, who became emperor in 31 B.C. at the age of thirty-one.

On March 17, 44 B.C., two days after Caesar's death, he presided over a meeting of the senate. He convinced the Senate to pardon the conspirators. They would be allowed to keep the public offices Caesar had given them. At the same time, Caesar would be honored and would receive a public funeral. All the measures Caesar had enacted, or had planned to enact, would be carried out.

The most powerful man in this new order was Marc Antony. Antony had been Caesar's closest associate and longtime friend. Shortly after the assassination, Caesar's wife Calpurnia let Antony take charge of Caesar's estate—his will, his private papers, his plans for future projects, and his great fortune. This position made Antony an important man.

Caesar's assassins had been officially pardoned by the Senate. But they soon learned that an official pardon was not enough. Many common people in Rome grieved over Caesar's loss and wanted vengeance. At Caesar's funeral, rioting

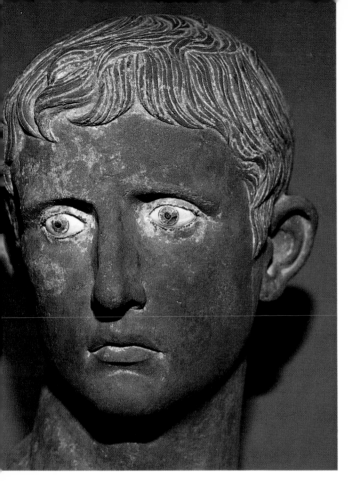

A bust of Octavian before his rise to supreme power.

With the conspirators out of the way, Antony had more room to strengthen his own hold on power. But he found he had an unexpected rival.

The rival was Caesar's principal heir—a grandnephew named Gaius Octavius, better known to us as Octavian. Octavian was the grandson of Caesar's younger sister, Julia. He was only eighteen, a student living in Macedonia, at the time of Caesar's death. Octavian was handsome, fair-haired, and well spoken. He was also sickly, plagued by a weak stomach and respiratory problems. Caesar had liked the young man and had given him a place of honor in his triumphal parades. In his will, Caesar adopted Octavian as his son and left him most of his fortune.

Octavian's parents and friends warned him against trying to collect the inheritance. Rome was a dangerous place for a man claiming to be Caesar's son. Even if he survived, he was much too young and inexperienced to play any important role in Roman politics. But in the spring of 44 B.C., Octavian went to Rome anyway. Within fifteen years, he had become the undisputed ruler of the Roman world.

The first step in Octavian's rise to power was to face Marc Antony. Octavian asked Antony to hand over the inheritance that belonged to him. Antony did not take the young man seriously and refused. Octavian then raised money on his own—enough to pay Caesar's bequests to the Roman people and to hold lavish festivals and games. He also raised his first army—an illegal one

broke out (perhaps spurred on by Antony). One of the causes of the rioting was the reading of Caesar's will. The people learned that Caesar had left each citizen the generous sum of three hundred sesterces, along with the public use of Caesar's gardens near the Tiber River. Angered by their loss of Caesar, a mob tried to burn the houses of the conspirators. One man was murdered because he was mistaken for one of the assassins.

The conspirators found it unsafe to remain in Rome. By summer of 44 B.C. they left Italy altogether, with Brutus and Cassius going on government business to the eastern parts of the Empire.

of three thousand soldiers. He had learned well from Caesar, whose power had rested on the support of the people and the control of an army.

Octavian also proved himself skillful at propaganda—communications that are geared for political ends. His greatest propaganda tool was his family name. As Caesar's adopted son, he began calling himself "Gaius Julius Caesar"—the name of his adopted father. Caesar's old soldiers rallied to that name. Civilians respected and feared it.

Antony, meanwhile, had grown unpopular with the Senate. They feared that he would become a dictator and take away their newly restored power. Cicero, who had praised Caesar's assassination as a blow for freedom, wrote a series of speeches against Antony. These were called the *Philippics*. In them, Cicero accused Antony of being stupid, a drunkard, and a tyrant. He begged Antony, "Try to make your brain work for a moment as if you were sober." He suggested that Antony should have been assassinated along with Caesar. The speeches angered Antony. He would one day make Cicero pay a terrible price for them.

The Senate became even more displeased with Antony when he raised an army against Decimus Brutus, now governor of Cisalpine Gaul. Antony wanted to be governor of the Gallic provinces himself; these regions would be a power base for his continued control of Rome. In early 43 B.C., Antony's armies had surrounded Decimus Brutus at Mutina in Cisalpine Gaul. The Senate needed a

tool to stop Antony. They found it in Octavian. Octavian seemed too weak to pose a serious threat to the Senate's power. But his ambition, and his magic name, could be useful against Antony.

The Senate sent Octavian, along with several Roman legions and the consuls for 43 B.C., to stop Antony's attack. The Senate promised Octavian money and land for his troops and the right to run for consul ten years under the legal age. In reality, they intended to give him nothing. As Cicero wrote, "We will praise and honor the young man, and then discard him."

The Senate had made a grave error. In April, 43 B.C., the armies of Octavian and the consuls defeated Antony at Mutina (the consuls themselves died in the battle and Antony escaped). But when the Senate refused to give Octavian what they had promised, Octavian marched on Rome. At the age of nineteen, Octavian forced the Senate to make him a consul.

This was only the beginning. To the horror of republicans (those who wanted the republic restored), Octavian soon made peace with Antony. Octavian met with him in November, 43 B.C., in Cisalpine Gaul. Along with them was Marcus Aemilius Lepidus, a former lieutenant of Caesar and now a leader of his own armies. The three generals—Antony, Octavian, and Lepidus—agreed to form a new ruling body called the Triumvirate. This body brought an end to the pretense of republican rule that had followed Caesar's death.

Like the so-called First Triumvirate,

The great Roman statesman Cicero opposed Antony and Octavian and paid with his life.

made up of Pompey, Crassus, and Caesar, this body exercised control over Rome's government. Unlike the First Triumvirate, the Second Triumvirate was formally approved by the Senate for a term of five years. Also unlike the first, this triumvirate held absolute power over Rome. Because Lepidus was politically weaker than the other two men, it was in effect a joint dictatorship of Antony and Octavian. Octavian had only just turned twenty.

The triumvirs wasted no time showing what the character of their government would be. They drew up a list of enemies, just as Sulla had done, and as Caesar had refused to do. Up to three hundred senators and two thousand equestrians were executed. At Antony's request, one of those killed was Cicero. His head and hands, the instruments of his powerful speeches and writings, were nailed to the speaker's stand in the Forum.

The only hope of republicans in Rome now lay in the East. There Brutus and Cassius, the leaders of the conspiracy to kill Caesar, were preparing for a last stand. Earlier in 43 B.C., the Senate had given them supreme command in the eastern provinces. They had gathered nineteen legions of soldiers at Philippi in northeastern Macedonia. Antony and Octavian prepared to fight them.

In October, 42 B.C., the opposing forces met. In the first battle of Philippi, Brutus defeated Octavian, but Antony defeated Cassius. In the confusion of battle, Cassius did not realize Brutus

had won, and he killed himself rather than be captured. Three weeks later, weakened by the loss of Cassius, Brutus again led his army to battle. Brutus lost, and like Cassius, committed suicide. Antony, who had once been friends with Brutus, took off his own cloak and used it to cover Brutus's body.

Caesar's assassination had finally been avenged. The last champions of republican rule were dead. The triumvirs settled down to divide the empire. Antony was by far the strongest of the three. He received control of the rich provinces of Transalpine Gaul and the East, including Egypt, Syria, Asia, and Macedonia. Octavian was given Spain and the islands of Sicily, Sardinia, and Corsica. Lepidus, who had been accused of disloyalty, was given the rebellious province of Africa.

In theory, Italy was to be shared in common by the three triumvirs as a place to raise troops. So was Cisalpine Gaul, which was now made part of Italy. But the only triumvir who was actually in Italy was Octavian. There he faced many unpleasant tasks. He had to find land on which to settle his veterans. He had to deal with famine and popular discontent. He had to deal with an enemy from his father's time—Sextus Pompey, the son of Pompey the Great, who was still fighting Caesarian rule. Sextus's pirate ships dominated the seas around Rome and interrupted Rome's grain supplies.

Antony, on the other hand, was having a pleasant time in the East. He collected tribute money. He reorganized

A Roman relief shows soldiers aboard a war galley. The vessel's long, curved bow was used to ram enemy galleys.

the provinces, setting up new client kings to rule as Rome's agents. He spent the winter of 4140 B.C. with Cleopatra, queen of Egypt. Cleopatra had been Caesar's lover; now she became Antony's. Cleopatra had learned that love was a good way to seal an alliance.

Harassed by problems in Italy, Octavian seemed to have the worst part of the bargain. But he knew that the seat of Roman power lay in Italy, not in the East. He was willing to suffer difficulties if they would make him stronger in the long run.

In 40 B.C., Octavian put down a rebel-lion by two relatives of Antony—Antony's wife Fulvia and his brother Lucius. That same year, Antony himself almost went to war with Octavian over the right to raise troops in Italy. The triumvirs narrowly avoided bloodshed, signing instead a new pact at Brundisium. To seal the agreement, Antony married Octavian's sister, Octavia. The Roman poet Virgil wrote hopefully that a golden age of peace was at hand: "All nature rejoices to see this glorious day." In fact, lasting peace would not come for years.

Antony and Octavian continued to

rule on separate sides of the Mediterranean Sea. Octavian, in the West, had been given new provinces to rule—Gaul and Illyricum—while Antony remained the master of the East. Both men were too busy to fight each other. Antony was preparing for war against the Parthian Empire. Octavian was preparing for war with Sextus Pompey, who had renewed his naval attacks on Italy.

Octavian was not a great military leader. But with the help of a former schoolmate and talented admiral named Marcus Agrippa, Octavian began to win victories. In 36 B.C., Octavian's fleet, led by Agrippa, defeated Sextus Pompey off the coast of Sicily. That same year, however, Antony lost more than twenty thousand men in a disastrous campaign against the Parthians. It did not matter that he later conquered Armenia, north of the Parthian Empire. It did not matter that Octavian himself had betrayed Antony by failing to send a promised army. Antony's reputation began to decline in the eyes of people back in Rome.

Octavian's great talent for shaping public opinion now came into play. He painted himself as the bringer of peace and prosperity to Italy, the man who defeated Sextus Pompey and rescued Rome's grain supplies. His reputation grew after the victories he won in Illyricum between 35 and 33 B.C. Antony, meanwhile, was painted as the loser against the Parthians.

Octavian also portrayed himself as an old-fashioned, patriotic Roman. He married Livia Drusilla, daughter of an ancient Roman family. He beautified Rome with public buildings. He supported artists and writers. And Octavian continued to trade on the name of Caesar. Since Caesar had been officially declared a god a few years earlier, Octavian called himself "Son of a God."

Octavian's greatest propaganda tool, however, was Antony's alliance with Cleopatra. After 36 B.C., Antony and Cleopatra started living together as lovers; she bore him three children. The alliance was one of mutual benefit. Antony needed the wealth of Egypt to finance his war; Cleopatra persuaded Antony to extend her domains. But there was also real affection between them. And Antony loved the Hellenistic culture of the East—a highly refined and luxurious way of life that combined Greek, Asian, and African influences.

Romans were suspicious of foreign influences and allowing women to hold positions of power. Octavian and his supporters used those fears to speak out against Antony. They said Antony was addicted to "Oriental," or Eastern, luxury. They said he was the plaything of Cleopatra. They called it an outrage when Antony divorced Octavian's sister. They claimed that Cleopatra wanted to rule Rome. Octavian even produced a will of Antony's—probably a forgery—showing he favored Cleopatra.

The Second Triumvirate, which had been renewed for another five years in 37 B.C., ended in 32 B.C. It was not renewed again. Octavian had already forced Lepidus out of the triumvirate and into retirement. Now he had only one other rival to defeat.

A later artist's idea of what the battle of Actium might have looked like.

In late fall of 32 B.C., Octavian de-clared war on Cleopatra. By attacking Cleopatra, he could attack Antony with-out being accused of starting a civil war. Antony and Cleopatra sailed to the northwest coast of Greece, along with a vast fleet and an army of thirty legions. Antony's main base was within striking distance of Italy. Octavian struck first.

Octavian's admiral Agrippa captured points along Antony's supply line. An-tony had to fight free of the blockade or be starved. On September 2, 31 B.C., in a naval battle near Actium, Antony's ships clashed with Agrippa's. It was one of the most important battles in Roman history. Had Antony won, the line of Roman emperors as we now know them might never have come into being.

Antony did not win. Little is known about the details of the battle, but Agrippa's navy easily defeated Antony's. Cleopatra and Antony escaped by ship to Egypt. Their enormous land army surrendered without a fight.

In August of the following year, Octavian made his way to Egypt to capture the fugitive leaders. He never found them alive. Antony committed suicide; Cleopatra did the same a few days later. Octavian spared their children to march as prisoners in his triumph. But he killed Caesarion, the reputed fifteen-year-old son of his adopted father Caesar and Cleopatra. Octavian wanted no one to challenge his hold on power—not even a half-brother.

At the age of thirty-one, Octavian was now the master of the Roman world. He had lied, betrayed people, and executed enemies to get there. But he had won. The civil wars were over. The republic was dead. The adopted son of Julius Caesar ruled.

The Emperor

Julius Caesar changed the course of Roman history. He brought an end to the decaying Roman Republic and replaced it with an autocracy, or one-person rule. He was a brilliant general, a skillful politician, a talented writer, a great orator. His conquests expanded Rome's empire. He showed greatness of spirit in pardoning many of his Roman enemies, even though this policy finally cost him his life.

But there was another side to Caesar. He was brutally cruel in wars against foreigners. He built up a huge personal fortune by taking property from provincials and sacrificing soldiers' lives. Above all, Caesar loved power. To make his power complete, he was willing to start wars and destroy an ancient system of government. The Roman Republic was not a true democracy, where the people rule. But it was at least based on law, peaceful debate, and the consent of many citizens. The government Caesar founded was based mainly on one man's will.

The men who killed Caesar tried to bring back the republic that had been destroyed. But Rome was still torn by faction, just as it had been before Caesar. Out of the factional fighting came a leader who was intelligent and ruthless enough to follow in Caesar's footsteps. Octavian made sure that Rome would never again be a republic.

Like his adopted father, Octavian founded an autocracy. But he designed this autocracy so that it would last for centuries. He knew that one of Caesar's great mistakes was his lack of respect for republican institutions. Octavian was more careful. In 27 B.C., Octavian officially restored the Roman Republic. From then on, the government was republican in outward form but autocratic in practice. In reality, the Roman republic was dead. The Roman Empire had begun.

The ruins of the Basilica Julia, begun by Julius Caesar in the city of Rome. In ancient Rome, a basilica was an open-air law court.

Shakespeare's Julius Caesar

The death of Julius Caesar has fascinated poets and artists from Roman times to the present. Perhaps the most famous version of the story is William Shakespeare's *Julius Caesar*.

Written about 1599, the play is a tragedy in verse form. Traditionally, a tragedy is a play about the fall of a person of high stature, such as a king or aristocrat. The hero has inner weaknesses that contribute to his fall. But the hero also shows courage and nobility in the face of defeat. In writing the play, Shakespeare had to decide who the "tragic hero" was. Was it Caesar? Or was it Brutus?

Shakespeare began the play where this book begins: the festival of the Lupercalia in 44 B.C., a month before Caesar's death. In the opening scenes, Cassius tries to talk Brutus into joining the conspiracy against Caesar. Cassius is angry that Caesar has become so powerful:

"Why, man, he doth bestride the narrow world like a Colossus, and we petty men walk under his huge legs and peep about to find ourselves dishonorable graves."

Cassius does not think Caesar deserves the high place he has reached. The dictator seems old, weak, and vain. He is afraid of Cassius but too proud to admit it. He turns down the royal crown, but seems slow "to lay his fingers off it."

Brutus, however, is a man of courage and integrity. He does not want to harm Caesar, but he wants Rome to be free. He thinks he can kill Caesar honorably, carving him "as a dish fit for the gods," not as a body "fit for hounds." He thinks the Roman people will welcome the assassination. But the people do not welcome it. And though Brutus's motives are noble, the murder of his friend Caesar, as seen on stage, is still horrible and bloody. Casca inflicts the first wound, shouting, "Speak, hands, for me!" Brutus inflicts the final wound.

Caesar's lieutenant, Marc Antony, is allowed to speak at Caesar's funeral. Antony succeeds in rousing the people to fury against the so-called "honorable men" who killed Caesar. Brutus and Cassius are forced to leave Rome for the East. In the play's final act, their armies do battle with those of Antony and Octavian. When the battle turns against them, the conspirators kill themselves. Brutus's last words are:

"Caesar, now be still. I kill'd not thee with half so good a will."

Antony is saddened by Brutus's death. The other assassins killed Caesar out of jealousy, while Brutus acted for what he thought was the good of Rome. Brutus, says Antony, "was the noblest Roman of them all."

The tragic hero of Shakespear's *Julius Caesar* is not Caesar at all, but Brutus—a good man who, rightly or wrongly, chose to kill his friend and master, and lost his life for it.

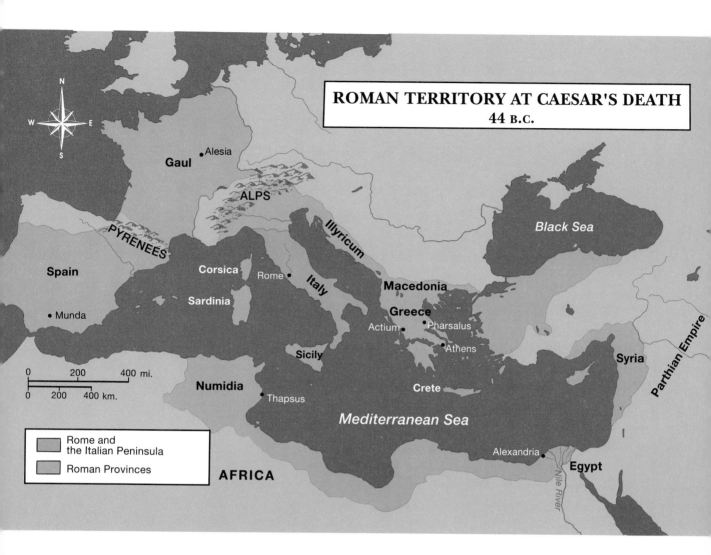

Gaul

•Alesia

ALPS

PYRENEES

Illyricum

Black Sea

Spain

Corsica

Rome •

Italy

Macedonia

Sardinia

Greece

• Munda

Actium •

• Pharsalus

Sicily

• Athens

Syria

Parthian Empire

Numidia

Crete

Thapsus

Mediterranean Sea

Rome and
the Italian Peninsula

Roman Provinces

AFRICA

Alexandria •

Egypt

Nile River

0   200   400 mi.

0 200 400 km.

Under this system, power supposedly belonged to the "Senate and people of Rome," just as it had for centuries. Elections for the full range of public offices were to be held every year. But real power was in Octavian's hands. His superior position was recognized in the title that the Senate gave him in 27 B.C.: Augustus. The word meant "majestic, dignified, holy." It is the name by which he is now best known. Like Julius Caesar's name, it was honored in the Roman calendar. The month in which Octavian conquered Egypt was eventually renamed "August."

Augustus Caesar was also given the name *imperator*, or commander-in-chief. Julius Caesar had also held the title, but Augustus made it his official *praenomen*, or first name. In time, it became the standard title for Augustus's successors. It is the root of our word *emperor*.

Augustus was also known as *princeps*, or first citizen. This title acknowledged

Portraits as Money

Roman coins usually featured an engraving of the current emperor. These portrait coins served an important purpose: In an era before modern means of communication like newspaper and television, they gave the inhabitants of Rome and its empire a chance to see what their rulers looked like.

Emperors were not the only members of the Roman world to appear on coins. The Romans admired the courage of Vercingetorix, leader of the Gauls, so much that they honored him with a portrait coin, despite the fact that he was Rome's enemy. Sometimes special coins were minted to mark a special occasion, like the coin shown on the contents page of this book—which commemorates the assassination of Julius Caesar.

The coins shown on these pages bear portraits of Rome's first emperors. This one depicts Augustus.

Tiberius, who ruled from A.D. 14 to 17 Augustus adopted Tiberius in the same way he himself had been adopted by Caesar.

Claudius. He became emperor in 41 B.C. after soldiers overthrew the cruel emperor Caligula, who followed Tiberius.

Nero, who became emperor in 54 B.C. following the assassination of Claudius.

his importance in the government without calling him dictator. It is the root of our word *prince*. The imperial system as founded by Augustus is called the "principate."

Over the years, the Senate gave the "first citizen" several official powers. For example, he had direct control of the important provinces of Spain, Gaul, and Syria, where most of the army was located. He had the right to speak first in the Senate. He had the powers of a tribune for life, which included the right to convene the Senate and introduce and veto bills. Most important, he had an unofficial quality called *auctoritas*, or prestige. This meant that Romans owed him honor and should carefully consider his advice. In practice, they almost never went against his "advice."

Augustus acted courteously toward the Senate. He led a simple home life. But underneath the outward show, Augustus was in fact the absolute ruler of Rome. Few people dared to challenge his decisions. For those who did, there was always the possibility of being executed or banished as a traitor.

Augustus ruled wisely. He reformed the administrative structure of the empire and made the economy stable. He founded more colonies in the provinces, added new territories, and made peace with the Parthian empire. A strong navy kept the sea free of pirates. A growing system of roads encouraged trade.

The result was a period of security and prosperity within the empire that is known as the *Pax Romana*, or Roman peace. This peace, which lasted about two hundred years, was not perfect. Democratic government did not exist. Any rebellions against Roman rule were crushed. For peasants and slaves, life was as hard as ever. But the civil wars of the late republic were over. The middle and upper classes prospered. A unified Mediterranean civilization was able to take shape. This period of peace was important for the future of the whole Western world. Under the Pax Romana, the rich heritage of Greek and Roman culture was extended and preserved for future generations.

Augustus was not a king, but nearly everyone expected him to name a successor, and he did: his stepson Tiberius. When Augustus died in A.D. 14, Tiberius became the second Roman emperor.

The line of Roman emperors lasted about five hundred years. Each emperor was given the titles "Caesar" and "Augustus," but none except the first Augustus was related by birth to Julius Caesar. Sometimes soldiers rose in revolt and made a general into an emperor. Sometimes an emperor peacefully chose a successor from among his relatives or associates.

In time, the Roman Empire weakened and fell. Many factors played a part in its decline. Among them were an overtaxed economy, too few men for the army, and invasions by migrating tribes. In A.D. 476, the last emperor of Rome, Romulus Augustulus, was forced from his throne. But for several centuries, the system founded by Augustus had brought peace and stability.

Julius Caesar was assassinated because he had openly taken away Rome's liberty—the freedom of Romans, especially noble Romans, to govern themselves. Augustus succeeded because he took away Rome's freedom more quietly. He made it seem as though the republic still lived, when in fact it had long since died. Augustus gave Rome peace and prosperity. The price that Rome paid was its liberty.

INDEX

Page numbers in *italics* indicate illustrations

SUGGESTED READING

Bowder, Diana, ed. *Who Was Who in the Roman World*. Ithaca, N.Y.: Cornell University Press, 1980.

Bradford, Ernle. *Julius Caesar: The Pursuit of Power*. New York: William Morrow & Co., 1984.

Bruns, Roger. *Julius Caesar*. New York: Chelsea House, 1987.

Caesar. *The Conquest of Gaul*. S. A. Handford, trans. New York: Penguin Books, 1982.

Forman, Joan, and Harry Strongman. *The Romans*. Englewood Cliffs, N.J.: Silver Burdett, 1977.

Gelzer, Matthias. *Caesar: Politician and Statesman*. Cambridge, Mass.: Harvard University Press, 1985.

Grant, Michael. *The World of Rome*. New York: New American Library, 1960.

Shakespeare, William. *Julius Caesar*. S. F. Johnson, ed. New York: Penguin Books, 1971.

Starr, Chester G. *The Ancient Romans*. New York: Oxford University Press, 1971.

Suetonius. *The Twelve Caesars*. Robert Graves, trans., Michael Grant, ed. New York: Penguin Books, 1979.

Picture Credits

The Ancient Art and Architecture Collection
(Ronald Sheridan Photo Library): 7, 10, 12, 14, 16, 17,
19, 39, 46, 55, 58-59.
The Bettmann Archive: 50.
Library of Congress: 9, 25 26 (both), 28, 30, 51.
Mary Evans Picture Library: 8, 13, 20, 22, 31, 33, 34, 36,
37, 40, 41, 42, 45, 48.

About the Author

George Ochoa received a B.A. from Columbia University and a M.A. in English from the University of Chicago. He has written *The Fall of Mexico City* and *The Fall of Quebec* in the *Turning Points in American History* series. He is the co-author, with Melinda Corey, of *The Man in Lincoln's Nose* (Simon & Schuster, 1990) and *The Book of Answers* (Prentice-Hall, 1990). *The Book of Answers*, about the New York Public Library's Telephone Reference service, is a selection of the Quality Paperback Club and the Book of the Month Club.